Judaism
This Is Our Faith

by Ronne Randall

Published in 2026 by Ruby Tuesday Books Ltd.
Copyright © 2026 Ruby Tuesday Books Ltd.

Editor: Mark J. Sachner
Design & Production: Tammy West

Photo Credits:

Alamy: 4 (Shotshop GmbH), 8 (Richard Levine), 11T (Adam Bronkhorst), 13L (Godong), 14R (Ilan Rosen), 15C (Vetre Antanaviciute-Meskauskiene), 18 (Eitan Simanor), 19 (Des E Gershon); Dreamstime: 15C (Rafael Ben Ari); Freepix: 5; iStockPhoto: 20 (grahamandgraham); Shutterstock: Cover (Famveld), 1 (tomertu), 6L (Oliver Denker), 6R (Philli), 7T (Olga Mukashev), 7B (Dragen Zigic), 9 (BBA Photography/Ryzhkov Photography/WithianCH/Pixel-Shot/Moiz 8006), 10 (Monkey Business Images), 11BL (Yes Photographers), 12L (Godongphoto), 12R (Barbara Ash), 13R (Elena Rostunova), 14L (Roman Yanushevsky), 15BL (tastyfood), 16 (HannahRuthBanana), 17 (ungvar/New Africa/etorres/Rui Elena), 21T (Mick Harper), 21B (Costin Constantinescu), 22 (maximpolak), 23L (Evgeniy pavlovski); Steph Sorenson Photography: 23R.

British Library Cataloguing in Publication Data (CIP) is available for this title.

ISBN 978-1-78856-211-9

Printed in Malta by Gutenberg Press

www.rubytuesdaybooks.com

Contents

Words shown in bold in the text are explained in the glossary.

This Is Our Faith

Judaism is a faith that began nearly 4000 years ago.

It began in the part of the world that we now call the Middle East.

People who follow this faith are called Jews.

Jews live all over the world.

The symbol of Judaism is the Star of David. In the **Hebrew** language, it is called the Magen David, which means "Shield of David". Hebrew is the language of Jewish prayer.

Jews believe in one God and that Abraham was the first Jew. Abraham promised that he and his descendants would worship only one God.

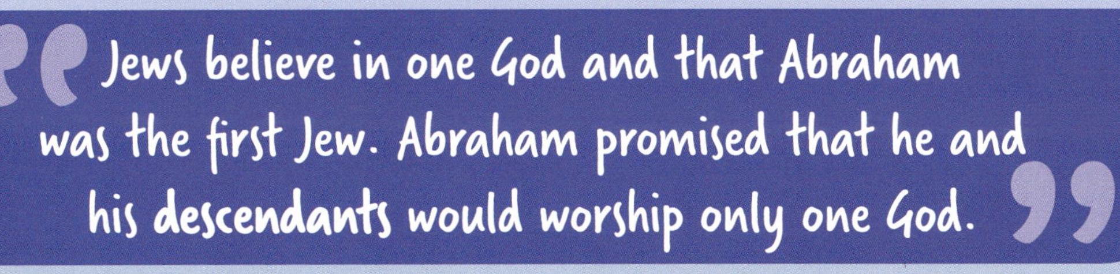

Abraham making a promise to God.

Abraham's agreement with God is called a covenant.

The Jewish Bible

The most important Jewish holy book is the **Torah**. It contains the Ten Commandments and many other laws.

Jews believe God gave these laws and Commandments to the **prophet** Moses on Mount Sinai.

"The Ten Commandments were carved by God on two stone tablets. Moses carried them down from Mount Sinai."

The Torah is a **scroll**, written on **parchment** in Hebrew.

The Torah makes up the first five books, or parts, of the Jewish **bible**. Later, more books were added.

The whole Jewish bible is called the Tanakh.

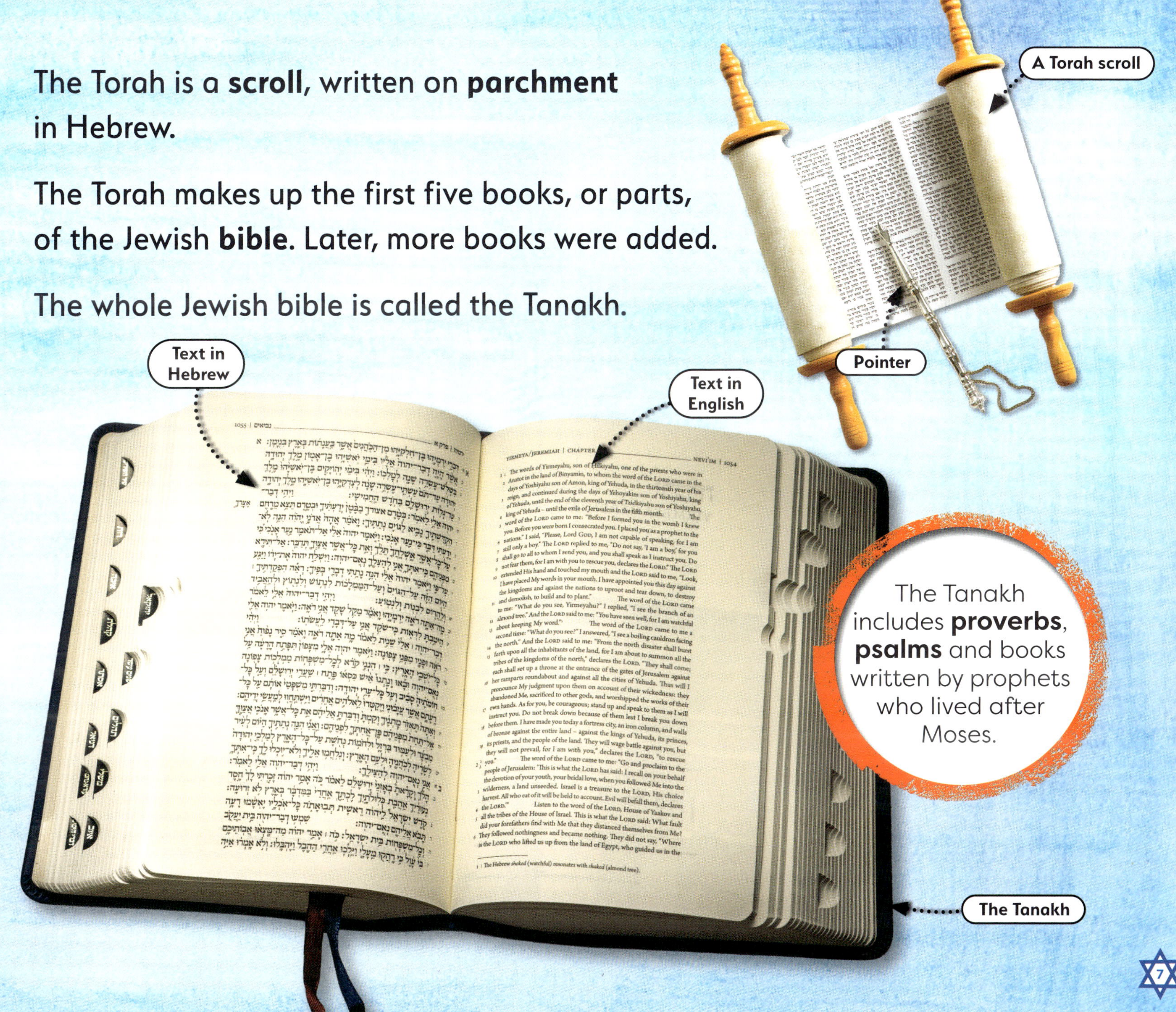

What Jews Believe

Jews believe in following the laws in the Torah, such as treating people kindly.

Jews must also do good deeds, like donating, or giving, to charities.

These young people in the United States are helping to pack bags of food for families who don't have enough to eat.

When I do a good deed, I am helping to make the world better. This is called tikkun olam, which means "making the world whole".

Some of the laws in the Torah are about food and eating.

Chicken soup with matzah balls (dumplings)

Falafel

Hummus

Brisket (slow-cooked beef)

Bagels with cream cheese and lox (smoked salmon)

Food that is okay for Jews to eat is called kosher. Only certain kinds of meat and seafood are kosher.

Shabbat

The Sabbath, or Shabbat in Hebrew, is the most important day of the Jewish week.

Shabbat begins at sundown on Friday and lasts until sundown on Saturday.

On Friday night, families and friends gather to welcome Shabbat.

They light candles and say **blessings** over wine and specially-baked bread called challah.

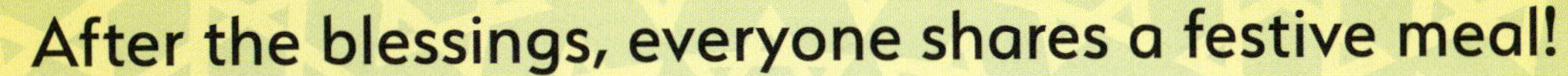

After the blessings, everyone shares a festive meal!

Shabbat is a day of rest, when no work should be done.

During Shabbat, many Jews go to **synagogue** to pray.

Challah

Welcome to a Synagogue!

Jews come together to worship in a synagogue.
They pray, sing and read from the Torah.

Services may be led by a rabbi,
which means "teacher".
However, anyone can lead a service.

A synagogue in London

A Rabbi reading the Torah

When they pray, men and some women wear a head covering called a kippah. They may also wear a prayer shawl called a tallit.

The most important object in a synagogue is the Torah.

It is kept in a special cupboard called the Holy Ark.
Above the Ark is a light called the Ner Tamid.

A Torah scroll is protected by a beautiful decorated cover and ornaments.

The words Ner Tamid mean "Eternal (forever) Light". The light reminds us that God is always with us.

Let's Celebrate! Passover

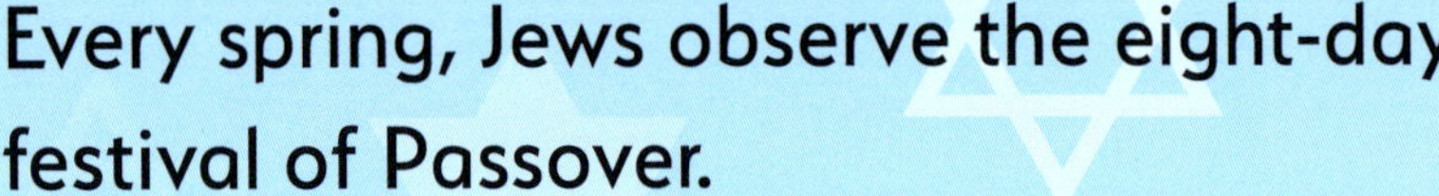

Every spring, Jews observe the eight-day festival of Passover.

On the first two nights of Passover, families and friends gather for a meal called a seder.

In the Passover story, long ago the Jewish people were slaves in Egypt. Passover celebrates their being led to freedom by Moses.

During Passover, Jews do not eat bread. Instead, they eat a flat crispbread called matzah.

Matzah is a reminder that when the Jews fled Egypt, they had no time for their baking bread to rise.

People sing songs, say blessings and read the story of Passover from a book called the Haggadah.

A special seder plate holds **symbolic** foods that tell the Passover story.

Let's Celebrate! Chanukah

In December, Jews celebrate **Chanukah** for eight nights. Every evening, people light one more candle. On the last night, all the candles are lit.

Chanukah is also known as the Festival of Lights. It celebrates a **miracle** that Jews believe happened 2000 years ago.

> When enemy soldiers ransacked the Jewish Holy Temple, Jewish rebels called Maccabees took back the Temple.

> The Maccabees found only enough oil to relight the temple's holy lamp for one day. Miraculously, the oil lasted for eight days, so there was time to get more.

Jews celebrate the miracle of the oil with presents, parties, games and special food.

The eight-branched candlestick is called a menorah, or chanukiah.

The shammas, or middle helper candle, lights the others.

Children receive foil-covered chocolate money called Chanukah gelt.

Children play a game with a spinning top called a dreydel.

People eat doughnuts and potato latkes (pancakes) that are fried in oil. These foods are a reminder of the miracle of the oil.

Happy Chanukkah

New Baby Celebrations

A new baby boy is named and welcomed to the Jewish faith at a brit milah.

The ceremony takes place when the baby is eight days old.

Jewish babies are given an English name and a Hebrew name that usually honours an ancestor or older relative.

A baby girl is welcomed with a ceremony called a simchat bat.

This takes place soon after the baby's birth.

A simchat bat in a synagogue in Solihull, UK.

Celebrating Bar and Bat Mitzvah

When a Jewish boy is 13, he becomes a bar mitzvah. A girl becomes a bat mitzvah at 13, or sometimes 12.

At a ceremony in their synagogue, the young person reads aloud from the Torah for the first time.

The ceremony is also called a bar or bat mitzvah.

After the synagogue service, there is a celebration kiddush, or lunch.

A family celebrating in Israel

Sweets and treats at a bat mitzvah party!

In the evening, family and friends enjoy a party with food, music, dancing and lots of fun!

Welcome to a Jewish Wedding

At a Jewish wedding, the bride and groom stand beneath a chuppah, which symbolises the roof of their future home.

A wedding in Israel

The couple sign a contract called a ketubah, promising to be faithful and kind to each other.

This bride, groom and guests are members of a community of Hasidic Jews. Their teachings and beliefs come from centuries of Jewish **traditions**.

At the end of the ceremony, the groom stamps on a glass. Everyone shouts, "Mazel tov"!

The broken glass reminds Jews that even at joyous times there is sadness in the world.

After the ceremony there is a celebration meal and dancing.

During a dance called the hora, the guests lift up the bride and groom on chairs.

Dancing the hora

A wedding in the United States

GLOSSARY

bible
A single holy book made up of smaller books, or parts. A bible contains stories and teachings about God and how people should live.

blessing
A prayer asking for God's love and protection.

Chanukah
An eight-day holiday celebrating the Jews' retaking their temple during a conflict 2000 years ago. You may sometimes see Chanukah written as "Hanukkah".

descendant
A relative who lives in a time after you.

Hebrew
The ancient language which Jews use for reading the Torah and praying, and which some speak every day.

miracle
Something amazing that seems impossible, but which some people believe really happened.

parchment
Thin sheets of leather-like material.

prophet
A person chosen by God to be a messenger on Earth. Prophets share God's words and teachings with other people.

proverb
A short saying (or sentence) that gives us advice or teaches us a life lesson. For example, "a cheerful heart is good medicine".

psalm
A song, poem or prayer that a person sings or says when worshipping God.

scroll
A long piece of parchment with writing that is read by unrolling it little by little.

symbolic
Standing for something else – for example, a heart shape is a symbol for love.

synagogue
A building (or place) where Jews gather to worship God, learn, celebrate and spend time with their community.

Torah
The most important book of the Jewish bible. In a synagogue, the Torah is usually written on a scroll.

tradition
Something that people have been doing for a long time, such as celebrating a particular festival.

INDEX